STROKES OF SOLACE

Poems

Photo Ramesh Singh

STROKES OF SOLACE

Poems

SANJEEV SETHI

CLASSIX

CLASSIX
New Delhi | Calcutta

Published by CLASSIX (an imprint of *Hawakal*)
70 B/9 Amritpuri, East of Kailash, New Delhi 110065
33/1/2, K B Sarani, Mall Road, Kolkata 700080, India

info@hawakal.com
www.hawakal.com

First edition July 2022

Cover designed by Bitan Chakraborty

Typeset in Adobe Garamond Pro (12 pts) & Tarjan Pro (14 pts)

Printed & bound in Thomson Press (India) Ltd, New Delhi 110020

ISBN 978-93-91431-26-6 (Paperback)

Price: USD 16.99

For
Namita Gokhale

Wingspan
Vibes to now
Thank you

By Sanjeev Sethi

Suddenly for Someone (1988, Atma Ram & Sons, Delhi)
Nine Summers Later (1997, Har-Anand, New Delhi)
This Summer and That Summer (2015, Bloomsbury, New Delhi)
Bleb (2021, Hybriddreich, Scotland)
Hesitancies (2021, CLASSIX, an imprint of Hawakal, New Delhi, and Kolkata)

Forthcoming

Wrappings in Bespoke (2022, The Hedgehog Poetry Press, UK)

ACKNOWLEDGMENTS

Stand Magazine, The Fortnightly Review, Erbacce Journal, The Recusant, Litter Magazine, Beir Bua Journal, Amethyst Review, Lothlorien Poetry Journal, Stride Magazine, Dreich Magazine, The Hamilton Stone Review, The Packingtown Review, North Dakota Quarterly, Talking Writing, Mad Swirl, Empty Mirror, K'in Literary Journal, Pomona Valley Review, Right Hand Pointing, The Dillydoun Review, Ancient Paths Literary Magazine, Roi Fainéant Press, Life and Legends, Sparks of Calliope, First Literary Review-East, Haikuniverse, Futures Trading, Former Cactus, After the Pause, Pyrokinection, Amphora Magazine, Otoliths, Meniscus, Rochford Street Review, Noon | journal of the short poem, Sledgehammer Lit, Outlook Magazine, Kavya Bharati, Ethos Literary Journal, Cafe Dissensus Everyday, Coldnoon, and Poetry Conclave Anthology.

Contents

Transcendence

The scenery is a set piece.
Crescent moon
in cardboard:
a window
with campestral settings.

The spotlight ushers me
into monologue mode.
I stutter: scream.
I speak to no one.
Not even myself.

On my own
with the page
they aren't velleities.
This handiwork of happiness
turns it for me.

LEITMOTIF

Tessera from our mosaic coruscates as the conversation encourages a crosscut and annuls the accord I had signed with myself. Misgivings hide us from ourselves: slaphappy, another phiz unveils itself.

As quelling of consciousness begins: it is easier to maul formulations of philosophy than issues of exchange and expediency. Emotion like an egg must cease or create: the quiet of your thought must question me.

DISTICH

1

Happiness has hierarchies
death is democratic.

2

Words are never said.
You're always told.

3

Never buy expensive diaries.
You will rarely use them.

4

Don't love too much
love correctly.

5

Empathy without experience
is climax without coitus.

6

Poetry is born
of unsettled scuffles.

7

Surfeit never satisfies,
it enlarges the exactness.

8

If you raise your voice too much
you will be co-opted or killed.

9

Money insulates
wealth secludes.

10

Hands skitter on an oiled body
as moonshine moves the mind.

Reliance

Yesterday informed me of a morrow
with no sunlight. In this ill-timed
ingathering duds outplace dividends.
Artistic aura negates the course for me.
When the unexpected crosses my curve,
I sift: crevasses are a part of the sketch
of my inhabitancy. Slights leave me
loose. His lambency counters the cue.

Fluctuations

On happy days why do I write
lugubrious lines?
Why is the heart leadfooted?
Why am *I me*?
A fluttering sheaf of papers
invites me to mimic
the mulligrubs.

I prorogue it to another clock.
Sadness does this.
It pulls you to its entrails,
inveigles you
to marinate in its spice
until another phase snaps
you out of it.

Patterned

Excess in the footsteps of future
slip and spill as the cut glass of
feelings inhale and exhale.

Your toe on the slate of my foot
scrawls alphabets I can't infer. My
body molds me into an ink slinger.

Carrying the candies of childhood
to our parleys delivers some distress:
allyship of a certain actuality.

Lulled by love? You probably are
acquiring another tongue, preparing
for another podium.

VOICE

Imagination facilitates
to capriole barriers set
by birth and its concomitants.
When ammo of invention
hurls at the dartboard
of jaded designs
they ride in opportune directions.

Comfort of conscience
sanctions thought
to marinate
in the sauce of ideality
while images
underwrite processes
with cerate of catchwords.

Redaction

An old hand
at grammaticide
Grammarly
buttresses him to bark
at whoever like
another cornered
in fume and flame
is energized to shriek
at the sight
of a fire-fighter.

In the Neighborhood

You let wounds stir-fry in your inner wok. If only
a willing one had sampled your nosh, its stench
would not have sullied you and stopped decibels
of silence from wiping out. The trail of your sorrow
will quell tardily as engrams sequester the frailties
of your act. No ache is as incisive; it needles one
to embroider one's endnote. If only alembic agencies
had prevented you by asking: why this haste?

Cyclicality

The slipway
cloaks my contusions.
It's an easy catch:
scrubbing
takes care of the sogginess.

I soak the pillowslip
an hour before
the help's appearance.
She rinses and restores
its original state.

TRANSIT

Pointless in squabbling about the window seat
in an airbus or van, look for one's inner lucarne.

Nutant or a crisp nosegay? Answer is crystal
clear. If every case had such an easy comeback?

Beyond velitations, ben trovato is balustrade
for a few to carry on. Aisle isn't for everyone.

FALLOUT

"I am no longer a toper." is my audible retort
to the proprietor of the ear-popping bar to his
energetic salaam and inquiry of me no longer
being a habitué. Processing me, his eyes pan
to the next patron: his gestures forfeit their fire.

MÉTIER

Unevenness is one marker of tides;
the other is contumacy of their craft.
The ocean slithers from side to side.
Whenever it badgers me, it frames
another stich on the shore of my burn.
Attitudinizing is an offshoot of fear.
Ferocity with which your flashback returns
makes me mull: why do we thrive in thought?

One can't be emotional about fiscal interests:
mislaid concerns incite cricks and confusion.
Inditing is an art form.
Talking about it tapers its impact.
Let the reader inhale its intensity.
Chinfests suit cinema.
They need the numbers.

META

Paraphrases of the past invite me
to a buffet of desserts. I rebuff the
offer. Gilded delineation in aphotic
sequences may have visual grace
but speculative episodes aren't for
me. I seek no mid-term exam. Each
sunrise-to-sunset, I test myself. My
faith requires no visa. It carries me
sans authentication.

THE NUT GRAPH

Fjords of desire are in a reliquary.
One survives on ceremonies.
A harvest forages for some time,
rich outturns render some more.

Sunlight has its shortcoming.
I saw the weaning away of our
lariat before we were cuffed
by circumstances.

Didn't want to destabilize the set-up,
waited for it to wash away. Words let
up when wounds weep, hanging like
tousled passages of a soiled text.

POV

Markers of gaze:
one is a nationalist Hindu
other a standpat Christian
another a fanatic Muslim.
Labels mock the one who isn't us.

Soft on self:
the others are snafued.
Wholeness is a cuss word:
in sect or segmentation
there is splendor.

In this frame:
bumbershoots slay
us with perforations.

CHRONICLE

Never orgulous
of one's orbit,
always on spec.
It's nothing like
what is on the screen
or telly.
The terrain is rugged,
shoulder is frozen.
I grow home
in heartland of demurrals.
Paragraphs of pamphlet
are orchestrated
by the quill of iffiness.
'*No comments*' obscures
a string of squibs.
In camouflage is continuation.

ARRANGEMENT

Some are pushing up daisies.
Others are stiff
due to ideology or intention.
This march has no music.
The band is over.
One is guarded
to get-together another one.

If you wish others
to walk on air for you,
they need to be subsumed
by pecuniary inflows or possessions.
Self-actualization bids
offer goose eggs to others.
On this path: seclusiveness is skywritten.

The Ticket

From the fringe,
I never had to squint
at the fluctuations,
plotzing spoke up for me.

Offbeat patterns find no patrons.
Such an ordinary line,
but if it clipped your cloth,
you may think otherwise.

Stains often announce
other sweeps. One needs no
zetetic formulations to follow this.
Tag along the windings.

Ana

As inanition takes over
I withdraw into words.
They inveigle me
with their richness
and resolve.
Who in the sublunary state
isn't for their lavishness?
When your namesake
doesn't quicken me,
I know it is over.
Fallout of feelings
cumulate at the poetic canon.

DECEPTIONS

He was born to a warlock.
As he grew, he gathered:
his spellbinder of a progenitor
was no prophet.

This bred trepidity.
His bête noire:
other's snitching on
his father's subterfuge.

If a voice had whispered: all
elders are enchanters. You, too,
will equip yourself with artifice.
Peg this on charm or conjury.

SACREDNESS

With confidence you tossed, *you're a*
tough customer, a tough customer as
if repetition settles it. I wanted to urge
you to change your gaze, clean the filter
but didn't, as raging parleys go nowhere.

Not a block or barrier when there is no
solution in sight, it's best to bequeath it
to registers of religiosity.

DECATHEXIS

In long-established fasteners
of familial zippers,
my aloneness leaves me unfurled.
We are so easily robbed
when we give ourselves to others.
Who will want to be a professional boxer
if epistaxis is the only reward?
When kindness is home,
no-one eyes the egress.

Observation

Post the onfall of the pandemic
approval ratings of
poetic webinars are on the rise.
The other night on
a streaming service
a volley of global voices
captivated me with their craft.
While leave-taking
a thought cruised my circuitry:
barring the host
poets ran with *short*
to singularize their contribution.

ALBUM

Through your harmonies, I have been able to touch
the hoofprint of your tenderness. The fragility
of your fear grabs me. We have a generation
between us. Time hasn't altered anything. You have
to wear your garment of grief; I have to wear mine.

Now and then, a breed of stallions kickoff their tantivies
on the bridle path of polymorphism. The manners of mating
are perilous. Our placement keeps us as kleptomaniacs
in the emporium of love. Shortages do this: perception
of chronic shortages more so.

BOOTSTRAP

You may have leaped
out of your creator
accoutered in correct syllables
and calming inflections.
For the rest, it's a grind.

Lapidary lines aren't duck soup.
Incubation aids the outcome.
Never dread the domineering.
Insecurities express themselves
in arrogancy.

When robbed of natural jewels
all joys are under-sized.
Equilibrium is in acquiescing:
conscience-stricken,
not self-condemnatory moves.

Fen

We mate like mannequins on
the shop-window of dreams.
There is a cutoff point
to skin extending itself.
If it is mine,
it will wrap around me.

Molters exist in another order.
Dermoplasty is for some.
Do those incarcerated
for immorality, retain the right
to take a position
on conscientiousness?

Silence

Uncial letters announce it. Even a jackass
gets it. Her pain, his pain, and in some ways
mine: catenation of a twenty-four-year copula.
The third stage, that dire C infests her, medico
gobbledygook warns us. Ambages are out:
I acquaint my maid's son of my readiness
to underwrite the procedure. Her eyes sign
her thank-you note.

SNIPS

1

Power to choose
is a flawed concept.
In its core is a corrupt gene.

2

You know you're aging when the anchor
you have been glued to starts graying.

3

Rain helps
answering
unanswered questions.

4

Words fail when
internal juxtapositions
find an outlet.

5

Backwash of your image brings in
new ones. You are a news channel
on desktop of my mind.

6

That time of year
editors nudge me
to mop your montage.

7

At dressage
trainer's untutored tongue
breaks in.

8

That was love alright
gaposis or not
you looked good.

9

A shorthand
of brisk emotions
is this love?

WISHERS

I was aiming to construct a universe without conditionalities but merchants have a unique way of allowing merchandise and its marrow to intervene. In such a setting, the thronged inbox announces a transoceanic email from niece. My birthday twin is three, his brother two years older.

On their cot clad in nightwear, they sing the natal day song on camera. A foliaceous mounting behind them beetling the world map adds another bend to background score. In sleety climes, this will quieten me.

Stop-Gap

Scramble for subsistence has an anagrammatic quality to it. To be a fluffer is as determined a course as any. To mass-produce emotions is unjust to all concerned. Most of all, to yourself.

A compromised mind requires no compensation. It is more threatening than an overwrought tellurian. If a misstep can raze a ratio, it isn't one. Justifications are just that: band-aids for a bother.

SUBTEXT

Vocabulary, as you and I
understand it, dissipates.
On the bedstead,
another one
direct and diaphanous,
begins its boogie.
The tone is irenic.

Sheets respond to alphabets
in calisthenic frames,
lisping unique cuneiforms.
Haptic sensations
accelerate the eagerness.
Breath decodes umpteen backronyms.
Outside the bedchamber,
the argot is empty.

Hoop

Sans cockade, we cruise along scraggy terrain
oblivious of the oppugn which runs the row.
Steers come by and by. When the equation
is emotional, pulchritude is not on purchase.

Volant emotions, if unsated, find acquittal
in stanzas. There is almost no deaccession
for books. The mangled are outcasts, like
lovers who have exhausted their animus.

Portamento

Bedewed groin at dayspring
corporeal blank call to love.

When you oil the system
be wary of skidding.

Friseur or fitter
will never be in the frame.

When you sulk; I wish I were
a crackerjack in zoosemiotics.

Laboratory of lazy lines
some fine ones set in.

Post power, they gain weight.
Flab isn't necessarily cellulite.

Don't evaluate every accomplishment
summative is freighted with substance.

CASUISTRY

Glottogony killed
whatever goodness we possessed.
Language assisted us
to hatch allowance,
ending the wholesomeness
of humanity.

Judicature, as in all systems
imbrued it with imperfections.
Purity is
for moral science practitioners:
who make known
from the margins.

Grief, when spilled,
is an incomplete story.
No one knows how much of it
is shared or shielded.
Legerdemain of locution
plagues us from the word go.

Comportment

Profusion exposes
its underbelly.
That is the nature
of excess:
it undresses in company.
To be silenced
is divinity's amercement,
more scathing the punition
severer the censorship.

Pasquinade by lover
is testimony
to troubled cross-pollination.
This is another kind of castigation.
Etchings don't ache.
They nick and nudge
the amour-propre:
like flickering lamps that keep alive
slipups in selection.

Vulneraries

Specious thoughts drive me through wayward
districts of wantonness.
In ravenousness, I purloin your pain.

There are spots for the whole schmear.
Professor's interpretation of his verse
is richer than a read of it.

Niche writing on a bestseller list secretes
an offensive smell, twinning effusive
salutations of a shopkeeper.

Whenever I call, I hear the ambient
clack and clatter of busyness,
isn't this enough to distract her?

PECCAVI

Thuribles of trust coax me to be myself.
In the calm of auroral currents, I inhale
without worry. In the noise of many
truths, I choose my assailants.

One's moral compass is as good as guilt
permits it. Whetted by His workbook,
outcomes are unwemmed, though our
daemon is lame as our lapses.

TERN

1

You blew up my bliss
in an incruent coup
quietly like a quilt with holes.

2

In the chime of your eye
I read the clef
egging you on to our chant.

3

When your partner looked
didn't look when I looked,
I knew he knew.

BIRTHDAY WISHES

Our chronology of chimes
began with brown
restive eyes making love
like liegeman of concupiscence.
Recension feeds as ravenously as this.

It hooks as when love
looked at me for the first time.
Stilb of a script must peal
with this postmark: soothe or singe
in carillon of longings.

Pointers

We must write the most laudatory validations,
present ourselves with the warmest certificates,
provide the best approval ratings. No-one else
is impatient to ratify our résumé.

In the grocery of my mind, I purchase sass and
serenity to grasp how to procure the right wares
for the right rewards. It's like being married to
a martinet: obey or opt-out.

Relay

Why do you shade your inner shrine?
My translator asks in a buddy-buddy
one-on-one. Direct paths are hardest
to handle, I tell myself.

In a flush of child-like avidity: I ask
him to cross-examine: put me through
the wringer. *Every question needn't*
be cashed; he soothes me.

From a Pistic Frame

There was no one to scumble
effusions of emotional strafe.
Connectives
through sentential etchings
altered my state.
Soon I sensed: lation of thought
is mightier than its impeller.

However meaningful a postulation
it's the outcome of an active mind
anatomizing a minuscule.
We are ill-equipped to sense
the supernal rota.
Allegiance to prie-dieu
leads to light.

Circa 1980

Palm tender like a poem tempts me
from incarceration of another ilk. I
place faith in the feel of your thumb:
on hoofs of haste as you hike pace
in the reined in milieu of bloom.

The affricate of joy has never been
as oozy. I'm a galoot. In multi-media
readings head turners score. In sooth:
there is no race, no perfect winner.
This isn't the Olympics.

Puzzler

We barebacked our way
to copse of roborant zeal
but in store were fallow seasons.
Negativity wears choker of
nervousness on her neck
to every gala of
the somatic kind.
No wonder I run away
from social routines.
Recoiling
is one way.
How does one persist
when nugatory colorants
are on the palette?

Numen

Inclemency turns on
the atmospheric pulse
to smudge the shift.
This isn't a taint.

When stars bounce,
you cannot bridle them.
At best, you can alter
future spins.

Forlorn edges, look for links.
Langue of family stings.
In numbness of inner self
fenestration aerates.

LORE

Sawdust of our first cabinet seesawed
any which way, piercing the eyes and
erasing magic of marigolds from our
midst. One good about the durational
gear, it helps in easing game plans.
We now order kitset and stuff.

Personalia

I negate the truths they tell me
about myself,
a trick I learned early in
game of one-upmanship.
Whigmaleeries twist on
the dance floor of inclinations,
I plié myself out of them,
an exercise practitioners
of the deadpan imbibe.
The closeness of tanzanite beads
crumble at the shrine of surmises.

Journaling

There is peace in pebbles. They rest
until reallocated. For the most part,
normal is a no-no. It is an invention
of the antinome lobby.

Hazing comes readily to teenyboppers.
If you hop six schools in six cities in
as many years there is reason to be
remonstrative.

While the elders click their flutes
and chime: *it is about adjusting and
making friends*, we stow away the
warps in our secret-sloop.

SUPPLICATION

In the unruliness
of my uppermost part
I draw on His omneity
to hush the house.
He is balm to bedlam
tune to soothing ribs
amidst turbulence.

I seek Him
in my lowest hour,
most luminous stretch.
This isn't for naysayers.
Bonus
is the belief.
There is no other benefit.

HETEROCHROMATIC

Hard-heartedness
is a malediction.
Let us locate the lens
to grief that has no lexicon.
No legs to stand.
Nobody to lean on:
a wail no one catches.

To cloak behind
hauteur of ratings
is a way to camouflage failings.
Let's be on the frontline.
Let our wares be marked
by myriad forces
for their true colors to flash.

DUOLOGUE

Perils in palaver:
while weaving a narrative
from the thesaurus of our minds
sometimes we lose sight
of the quintain.
Commas in conversation
grease the extemporization drive,
helping us ply little-known openings.

BALLOT

A flurry of footloose word-armies,
unleashed in makeshift assemblies,
impress at first blush. On jelling
for gravitas, one realizes, empty
words leave us unfurnished.

The familiarity of promise is like
an earworm. Takeoff on truism?
I wish I could urge them to hustle
with a new hook, bunko with a buss.
Lure me with unwonted lies.

TEST

Have you understood?
She nods.
Incorrect queries hustle
wayward returns.

A clearer picture emerges
on assessing
gauge of her grasp.
Conversance is multi-dimensional.

LIMPIDITY

Hat in hand
I genuflect
to the All Powerful:
sifting for His presence
within my perimeter.

I burnish
His simulacrum
with my being.
When I waver
I notice His need.

I wish there were real ways
of realizing Him.
A word of honor,
not the puff of texts.
I itch for His blacklist.

In Labial Communion

Stains on my lips
compelled my teeth
not to bow to the bleach of togetherness
as another charter hooked us.

In the interim
other drills ensued:
as mundificative realities beat
the rigidity of material exigencies.

Our season saw itself being denied
its domain as the aroma of your armpit
reached another nostril. All we possessed
were wallets with no cold cash in them.

FANCIES

Your annunciations
bestow their lyrics
to the jukebox
of justifications
as breath plays havoc
with their plans.

I bow to the celestial:
permit you to perform
like the wiliness
of an uncalled-for wish.

Maringouins couple
on my naked forearm,
their hochmagandy
a portraiture
of our tempo:
then and now.

Toss-Up

There are no marigraphs
to measure
the tides within me.
In my mind,
you're in a sunsuit.

Our energy fails
to move at another flush.
Even as the barchan
in my bubble spreads
to nothingness.

BEQUEATHAL

Uneven footprints ornament
the borders
of my bent.
Canned music follows
its cut.
In this din and declivity
I breathe.

Flat, mutual funds
and other farthings
will land at legatee.
My pangs and poems
aren't allocable.
They will surround
their landing-place.

Mantelpiece

The flowers of shame
preen in pottery.
Adjoining it, the miniature
firkin's emptiness
is evident.
I tell myself,
on ledge of life
there is no club
for the cursed.

Inexorability

You texted on my forearm
frames of our future now
WhatsApp me the Pope
on virtues of forgiveness.

The fallout of years:
the diminutive dulls.
Is it i or y in the pet name?
Stutters aid our speech.

The odd bird trills to itself
on the edges of its ether.
There is no sinfonietta,
no showgoer.

NIMIETIES

The mango melts
as easily as the ice
evaporates
in the warmth of my mouth.

Valentine's Day
recites its ritornelle,
annually in the foyer
of my oneness.

There is comfort in calories.

LIFEBLOOD

A prinker engages with temporal superficies. This is a middling slip-up in tourbillion of earthly spice. Why niggle? There are myriad graver misdeeds. Each has to charter an internal codification identifying with their whatness.

Whether in heather, ebony, or ivory the exogenous heads our selection. Someone may be a posthumous baby but no-one is born days after the demise of his or her birth mother. All this as polemics of equality are as old as Methuselah.

IMAGER

In the hearth of your bear hug: I thaw multiple
reminiscences. This tableau never calls off its
trajectory. Axioms have a way of annoying us
if we are on their opposite side.

In your saccade, a million new questions spur a
certain restlessness. Certitude kills, but uncertainty
prolongs it. My junket is an endless Jornada. Isn't
it de trop? This one is for the parched.

Shoo-In

The ersatz is a stand-in
when operatives
of the establishment:
cosmic or corporeal,
shy away from
offering authentic spells.

When commitment is on cue,
humor has a home.
We laugh at fiddle-faddle:
as douceurs, air the quality
of reception
in a dense watering hole.

A billet-doux in majuscule
balms no one: it asserts
the awkwardness of amour.
Feelings whoosh
without a vehicle:
those in line have the appetence to heed it.

Reprise

Love in our lexicon is an invective.
The wind rarely measures
up to my intent.
I clench an unlit candle.

The folds of your thighs
hold the secrets
even as eyebrows
caution me of my course.

Sunshine blunts our sight.
In the moonlight,
jewels within me glisten.
But there is no emptor.

Value on its own is valueless:
even as the one on the case
places the decimal
in an inaccurate spot.

In your arms, my strain erupts:
warmth incises onto misgivings.
I have held my quill
as long as I could.

USAGE

When a confabulation perches on an awkward crossway
with boyhood chums or a lover whose lane is no longer
a compulsion, I state with all the might I can measure up:
everyone has someone or the other on their map.

Post hoc, I seek eye contact. Most are rapt with the routine:
playing with the ice over their thirst quenchers or reading
messages on the mobiles. A few gaze vacantly at me.
Certain utterances: for the self.

ATTAINMENTS

At the end of our anthology, the ambient stir—
an expedition through wobbly terrain: like
one held captive before a buffet, not permitted
the courtesy of consumption. There is no-one
to implicate but my untutored heart and hungry
body. Each togetherness has a tenure. There is
grace in accepting it. In the shapelessness of
drifts, I see a silhouette: this is consciousness.

Book

My spine
on your shelf
in your profile picture
announcing:
I exist in your essence.

Or maybe outlying traces
do not irk.
That is the trouble
with speculative spurs
they never slake.

Deduction

Littleness is a supercilious lilt:
let it slide.

Your saining too filters in.
In your firmness
I seek solace from you.

Walking away from self
isn't as easy.

Allocating it to the Almighty,
and drawing a blank on our burden
is one way of styling the system.

The other is to offer answerability
for the environment.

LANDING

Self-starters usually get someplace. It's in
the order of things to be your intercessor.
If you wait for the wind to call out for you,
you will have to hang onto your headgear.

Still, a damp squib may cross your curve. A
well-lit map doesn't secure an easy ride. There
is no grubstake. No futzing around. In this
ticker-tape parade, a made man takes the lead.

MORALITY

Those who're in concert with all schools of music are with none in a go for broke sort of way. Or they are paltering. Excellence dwells in exceptionalism. There isn't one definition of privilege. It is a pivot of the panorama. Brusque interjections by the self to a well-thought-out spiel on future grooves leave me irate. It's like theodicy: it hurts no one except those who are in line for it.

SCORE

Two competing narratives of history
never meet up for a mug of java,
share their scrambles,
seek validation from the other.
All this as historiographers
are impatient to pan them
to this or that heading.
Narratives are static
until forces against their hegemony
gather momentum:
as is the case with latter-day brass tacks.

THREAD

Spoor of your silence reaches my cove,
urging me to hear your hymn. Conjoined
by the conception of pain, our scales are similar.
Lies that light up your stairwell are my untruths as well.

The curse of cover is a habitual offender, playing footsie
with such finesse, one has little choice but to relent.
Jigsaw puzzles are used as rails to energize our rallies.
Partners in another birth we will perdure.

Knock About

In brio of white heat
we miss memorializing
the portion is dwindling.
When patterns unfold
realization dawns:
we are spear carriers
of our sagas.

If we see ourselves
as viatores
on prolonged sallies,
proprietorial instincts
will be clipped.
This will foster
greater equitability.

MARGINALIA

On his forty-fourth, I am the first
ever to wish him, not his mate,
not his mother, nor his son or siblings.
In his cloche, there never was any cake.
No potlatch on his red-letter day.

His dreams subvocalize his failings,
fantasies are mute expressions
of potent fears. Somewhere in him
there is a bomb whose button he cannot find.
Even the robes he borrows have cuts bigger
than the foxholes, he longs for.

MINIATOR

In this microcosm
packed with people
I'm graded
to be my walking stick.
Silence unhinges incantations
that smoothen the crossings.

An unwritten handbook
within me reads the passage
required to arbitrate
my amble.
I surrender
to its shower.

BUZZCUT IN COVID-19

She removes the strap.
I have the shakes.
Vulnerability etches itself
on my irises.
This reminds me of a reversal:
as eide briefs us about another era.

PRIVITIES

I don't carry the conceit
of a rationalist.
I am conscious
of my condition.
I am a votary
of the Omniscient.

But my God
isn't for display.
He is not
a fill-in for fripperies.
There is no deity
on my draperies.

CHEF-D'OEUVRE

Raked on coals
by an unseen powerhouse
it seems I am always
in a sedulous cauldron.
Chefs of caliber
add merit and material
to create a masterpiece.
When visitants drop by
I garnish the viands,
with poise
and accept the praise.

JOLLIFICATION

This Yuletide, I'm again inbreathing
exhaust from begrutten flames. What
is it about fire? Spark or spontaneity?

Like a paleontologist, I wonder what
was there to us, to our togetherness:
forgetting we were other people then.

Buggered by the final arbiter, I have tried
to obliterate your eyes were home to my
emptiness: counterpane without peepholes.

STUBS

1

We become those in our growing years
we never wished to be.

2

In closeness, we distance parts of ourselves.
In some ways, only strangers know us.

3

I am willing to wind up connections.
Daub me in your color.

4

It isn't projection and puff, living
is delousing and dilemmas.

5

Thought to thoroughfare, peradventure to pernancy
conversations with *karma* lessen our smallness.

Finis

In din of my depository,
your darkness
sanitizes the space.
This is no hugger-mugger.
Eternal rest has integrity.
In a cosmos
where all are ready and ringent
to compromise
its resoluteness unnerves.
Fatality has no fall guy.
The finality of it all
fine-tunes bereavement.

NOCTURNE

Within an indicium
of imperfections
we have to seek
our peace.
If the search
is only for fault lines
our chase
will never cease.
It is the tempo
of waves
never to tire.
Altering tidelines
is their anthem.

June 2022

Decals of a decade
gone by stir up a salute
to orneriness of exposure.
While in its reach
there were other reverberations.

The edifice of shame is assembled
by those in superintendence.
It's to invalidate.
It may be due to fear or not fully
recognizing the ramifications.

A few slots from sixty
I ought to be an adult. I will bill
and coo with the windmills in my
inmost and position myself as my
own éminence grise.

PRAISE FOR SANJEEV SETHI

HESITANCIES

In *Hesitancies*, we find a complete poet whose wonderful passages frequent both the inner world and the outside one with remarkable ease. It is a collector's item and a must-read for all poetry lovers.
Aneek Chatterjee, *Colorado Review*, USA

One needs to admire Sethi's ability to say so much in such few words, and that is where the strongest point of this collection lies.
Namrata, *Kitaab*, Singapore

There is no one who writes like him, works as hard, or is as dedicated to his craft, and for that, I salute him.
Ghenghis O'Riordan, *Dreich Broad*, Scotland

The delicacy of style with a contemporary playfulness of themes and exquisite word-play makes *Hesitancies* a must-read.
Sutanuka Ghosh Roy, *Otoliths*, Australia

Sethi's sensibility is delicate and full of grace for the human condition. His poems call to readers with a quiet insistence, pulling us into matters of the heart and mind with the voice of a wise friend.
Cristina Deptula, *Synchronized Chaos*, USA

A reader of this volume will experience time-capsules of life and do so in a more profound way than he or she has ever imagined.
Amit Shankar Saha, *Compulsive Reader*, Australia

I savored every poem, every word, every thought and was dazzled by his mastery of the poetic craft.

Sapna Dogra, *Muse India*

His books should be read by everyone for the lessons and perspective they provide.

Nikita Parik, *Kavya Bharati*, India

BLEB

Sanjeev Sethi creates a monumental work of grace from raw feelings. These tiny gems cut to perfection show us that he creates a world that others take reams to describe.

Ra Sh, *Ink Sweat and Tears*, UK

His wistful and metaphorical writings have cemented his place as a true poetic visionary, and his collections are undoubtedly a symbol of his gifted abilities.

Balraj Sohal, *Desiblitz*, UK

This collection will light up inner and outer regions of existence—collective, individual, cultural, and spiritual.

Sunil Sharma, *SETU*, USA

Sethi's writing does not carry markers of his ethnic or cultural identities. I believe this is a hard-earned universality.

Shamayita Sen, *The Book Review*, New Delhi

Note: *Bleb* and *Hesitancies* were published a month apart in 2021.

ABOUT THE AUTHOR

Sanjeev Sethi has published six books of poetry. His poetry has found a home in more than 390 journals, anthologies, and online literary venues in over 30 countries. This includes *The London Magazine*, *The Fortnightly Review*, *3: AM Magazine*, *London Grip*, *Walleah Press*, *North Dakota Quarterly*, *Hamilton Stone Review*, *Indian Literature*, *and Outlook Magazine*, among others.

He is the recipient of the Ethos Literary Award 2022. He is the joint-winner of the Full Fat Collection Competition-Deux, organized by The Hedgehog Poetry Press UK. Sethi is part of the Highly Commended list in the 2022 Erbacce-Prize UK from among 15 thousand submissions. He lives in Mumbai.

Find Sanjeev Sethi:
Twitter @sanjeevpoems3
Instagram sanjeevsethipoems

www.ingramcontent.com/pod-product-compliance
Lightning Source LLC
Chambersburg PA
CBHW050021170726
48282CB00025B/500
* 9 7 8 9 3 9 1 4 3 1 2 6 6 *